Sheila Lane and M

Explorers' Stories

CAMBRIDGE UNIVERSITY PRESS
Cambridge
New York   New Rochelle
Melbourne   Sydney

Explorers' Stories

In the middle of the sixteenth century, monks are working on navigation charts in one corner of the library of San Pablo monastery, in Spain. They are plotting the routes of the great explorers. As they work, the monks imagine what life was really like on board the small ships called caravels that sailed the high seas between 1492 and 1522.

Each explorer's story is told as a play. The first is Christopher Columbus' voyage westwards across the Atlantic in 1492. Columbus is searching for a sea route to the fabulous East at a time when many people still believed that the world was flat.

In the second play, Vasco da Gama sails east, round the Cape of Good Hope, and then across the Indian Ocean, in another search for a sea route to India and fortune.

The third play is about Ferdinand Magellan, and the hardships suffered by the crew on their voyage. They sail round the southern tip of South America and across the Pacific Ocean, on the first circumnavigation of the globe.

The characters who take part in the plays are the **Playmakers.** The monks in the monastery library, who watch the three plays are the **Playwatchers.**

During each voyage, the passage of time is shown by the Recorder, who reads short extracts from the ship's journal.

Contents

PLAYWATCHERS

Spanish Monks

BROTHER FRANCISCO ⎤ two monks who are making maps
BROTHER PAULO ⎦ of the newly discovered lands
BARTHOLOMEW LAS CASAS – who printed the journals of the
explorers

The arena is empty, except for one corner, which is set up with a small table, maps, charts and a globe. The TWO MONKS *walk in, carrying some books.*

FRANCISCO   (*turning globe*) The world was a small place in 1492, Brother!

PAULO   But the oceans must have seemed enormous to the seamen in their little ships.

FRANCISCO   It was the King of Portugal, the one they call Henry the Navigator, who started it all. To him these great seas (*tapping globe*) were not a great barrier . . . but a highway.

PAULO   (*laughing*) But Henry stayed at home himself, in comfort!

FRANCISCO   But think how he opened up men's minds. Think of that first voyage . . . think of Columbus!

PAULO   There was a man of courage!

   (*Loud knocking is heard.* BARTHOLOMEW LAS CASAS *comes in and the two monks greet him.*)

FRANCISCO   Bartholomew Las Casas! Welcome!

PAULO   (*hopefully*) Have you brought the journal?

BARTHOLOMEW　You are eager, Brothers! (*showing book*) Look! (*reading from cover*) 'The First Voyage of Christopher Columbus'. (*looking up*) You will find that everything is most carefully set down, just as Columbus wrote it in his log.

FRANCISCO　(*opening book*) FRIDAY 3rd AUGUST 1492 – He writes, 'I set sail from Palos harbour . . . at eight o'clock and sailed with a strong breeze . . . in the direction of the Canaries . . .'

PAULO　(*impatiently*) Turn the pages, Brother! The route was known as far as the Canary Islands.

FRANCISCO　(*turning pages*) THURSDAY 6th SEPTEMBER (*reads*) 'Set sail from Gomera this morning and shaped the course for the voyage . . .'

PAULO　Ah! That's it! Think of the courage of the man – to set out across uncharted seas – with such a crew!

FRANCISCO　Look at this! (*reads*) 'We took our seamen from Palos prison, on the promise of a free pardon for their crimes . . .'

PAULO　(*laughing*) No wonder it's said that Columbus' crew were ex-gaol birds, future murderers and pick-pockets out of a job!

FRANCISCO　(*seriously*) The good Columbus had his Christian faith. Columbus was a man of God, Brother!

BARTHOLOMEW	Look! His ships are listed here. (*turning page*) 'Santa Maria, Pinta and Nina . . . with 88 men.'
PAULO	(*longingly*) How I wish that I'd been one of them!
BARTHOLOMEW	(*eagerly*) Brothers! Read this book . . . and go with Columbus in your imagination!
FRANCISCO	Ah yes! But from the safety of our library, here in Pablo!
PAULO	(*excitedly*) Let us imagine . . . (*running forward*) . . . that this great space is Santa Maria's deck . . .

(SAILORS *from first play quickly 'build' a ship shape with ropes and barrels.* (*see p.78*)

Here is the starboard side . . . (*walking over*) and here is the port . . .

Here begins the story of Christopher Columbus

Christopher Columbus

Playmakers

The officers

CHRISTOPHER COLUMBUS – Admiral, on the flagship, Santa Maria
ALONZO – Columbus' pilot on the Santa Maria

MARTIN PINZON – Captain of the caravel, Pinta
VINCENT YANEZ – Captain of the caravel, Nina

SEGOVIA – the King of Spain's Inspector
ESCOVEDO – the King of Spain's Recorder

The crew

BERNO
RODRIGO ⎱ seamen loyal to Columbus

RASCON
QUINTERO ⎱ seamen accused of damaging the Pinta

GRECO
CARLO ⎱ seamen who are reluctant to go on the voyage
FERNANDO

DOMINO – the ship's boy on the Santa Maria
Other sailors

The Route taken by Christopher Columbus in 1492

EUROPE

PORTUGAL
Lisbon SPAIN
Palos

AFRICA

Gomera
Canary Islands

ATLANTIC OCEAN

San Salvador

NORTH AMERICA

CARIBBEAN SEA

SOUTH AMERICA

PACIFIC OCEAN

SCALE

3000 MILES
2000
1000
0

LEAGUES
800
600
400
200
0

Christopher Columbus

MARTIN PINZON *and* VINCENT YANEZ *stride onto the deck of the Santa Maria.*

PINZON   Ho there, Yanez! Is the Nina ready to sail?

YANEZ   Ready to catch the morning tide. But what of the Pinta? Has all the damage been made good?

PINZON   The rudder's fixed and all the holes repaired. The Pinta's sound again.

YANEZ   Who did the damage? Do you know who the villains were?

PINZON   It can't be proved – but I've brought Rascon and Quintero over to join the Admiral's crew. Here, their movements can be watched.

(ALONZO *comes in and overhears.*)

ALONZO   Never fear! If those two so much as tamper with a splinter on this deck, I'll have them both in irons. Captains! Columbus has ordered all the crew to meet him here before we sail.

YANEZ   So that's the reason for our summons!

PINZON   What of the King's men?

YANEZ   Aye! What of Segovia and Escovedo? Are they summoned too?

ALONZO   (*hisses*) Keep your voices down! King Ferdinand's Inspectors spy at every keyhole. (*looking round*) They're coming now!

(SEGOVIA *and* ESCOVEDO *come in, followed by* SAILORS *who set to work on deck.*)

SEGOVIA   (*bowing*) Ah! Martin Pinzon, Captain of the Pinta! (*He bows to Escovedo.*) Who is the other fellow, Escovedo?

PINZON	(*opening Record Book*) Vincent Yanez! He is Captain of the Nina, Master Segovia.
SEGOVIA	Yanez! Ah yes! (*to Pinzon*) It has come to my ears, Martin Pinzon, that two of your men have holed your ship. (*nastily*) Why didn't you watch them? These repairs cost time and money, you know.
PINZON	From now on the remedy is in your hands, my Lords!
ESCOVEDO	How so?
YANEZ	Pinzon has brought the two suspects over to the Admiral's ship, to join the Santa Maria's crew.
PINZON	So, from now on, you can be Columbus' watch-dog on the pair of them. Come gentlemen! The Admiral has bid us wait for him here. Sit upon the deck . . .
SEGOVIA	Upon the common deck! I am the King's man. I've come on this . . . dreadful voyage . . . to be the Royal eyes and ears.
ESCOVEDO	And I, his hand.
YANEZ	(*throwing cloak over barrels*) Then sit upon my cloak! (*grinning*) Fit for King Ferdinand himself, my lords!
PINZON	(*quietly to Alonzo*) I don't envy Columbus, having these two upon his ship!
ALONZO	(*whispers*) Remember . . . they hold the purse-strings and will write reports upon us all.
	(COLUMBUS *strides in.*)
COLUMBUS	To you all, greetings!
ALL	Greetings, Lord Admiral Columbus!
COLUMBUS	Alonzo! You know my mind already. Get up to the bridge while I am here.
ALONZO	Aye, aye, my Lord Columbus! (*He hurries out.*)

COLUMBUS	(*to Domino*) Go with him, boy!
DOMINO	Aye, aye, Admiral! (*He follows Alonzo.*)
COLUMBUS	Tomorrow, September 6th, is the day. With a good north-east wind behind us, WE SAIL!
ALL	(*saluting with fists*) WE SAIL!
COLUMBUS	At day break we'll leave the shelter of these islands and sail towards . . . the East!
PINZON	To India!
YANEZ	And the East!
COLUMBUS	(*making sign of cross*) I pray God will guide us in our search.
SAILORS	(*all on one knee*) We pray God will guide us in our search.
PINZON	To India!
YANEZ	And the East!
SAILORS	(*rising*) To India and the East!
COLUMBUS	(*looking hard at sailors*) So . . . WESTWARD . . . HO!
GRECO	(*running forward*) Westward! NO! EASTWARD . . . my Lord Admiral!
COLUMBUS	Ah, no! We sail due WEST to reach the EAST.
	(SAILORS *mutter amongst themselves and look uneasy as* COLUMBUS *turns to Pinzon and Yanez.*)
	Is that not so . . . Pinzon? . . . Yanez?
PINZON, YANEZ	That is so, Columbus.
COLUMBUS	We sail WEST to reach the East, because it is my true belief that this world of ours is ROUND! So . . . one way to reach the East – is to sail WEST!
	(SAILORS *mutter more loudly and push Greco forward again.*)

GRECO	We heard some talk of this plan of yours, Lord Admiral, on the way out from Spain, but . . .
COLUMBUS	Forget your fears, Greco! This Earth of ours is ROUND. So, if we sail out towards the west, we'll reach the Indies, rich in spice and jewels, which lie there to our east!
GRECO	(*drawing back*) Sail WEST . . . to reach the EAST!
COLUMBUS	(*to sailors*) That is my resolve!
	(SAILORS *continue to mutter.*)
	You, Martin Pinzon – to the Pinta! Vincent Yanez – the Nina! Tomorrow we sail! From now on, we'll send word to each other on the line. Farewell . . . until we meet again . . . IN INDIA!
PINZON, YANEZ	IN INDIA, Columbus!
COLUMBUS	I'll to my charts and maps!
	(COLUMBUS *goes out one way, and* PINZON *and* YANEZ *the other. The* SAILORS *surge forward.*)
GRECO	So the rumours that we heard are true! We're to sail WEST!
CARLO	(*wildly*) Did you hear what he said?
FERNANDO	(*pointing to west*) It's the edge of the world – out there!
SAILORS	(*fearfully*) The edge of the world – out there!
GRECO	How can he KNOW that the world is round?
CARLO	(*wildly*) The earth is flat – we all know that!
FERNANDO	Nobody returns from the edge of the world!
SAILORS	(*fearfully amongst themselves*) Nobody returns – from the edge of the world!
GRECO	I don't believe it! The world's not round!
CARLO	(*wildly*) The world's not round – we shall all be drowned!

14

FERNANDO	What will happen to us if we go on?
SAILORS	(*amongst themselves*) What will happen to us?
	(SEGOVIA *and* ESCOVEDO *walk forward.*)
SEGOVIA	(*to Escovedo*) Their heads are full of ancient tales! (*to sailors*) What will be your fate if you put your feet back on Spanish soil? Have you thought of that? (*to Escovedo*) Escovedo! Read from your Record.
ESCOVEDO	(*reads*) 'From Palos prison there volunteered . . . Greco, a convicted thief . . . Carlo, guilty of attempted murder . . . Fernando . . .'
SEGOVIA	(*holding up hand*) Enough! Your fate, you fools, is gaol! Columbus took you from behind prison bars to go on this voyage. So shut your lips and set about your work! Come Escovedo!
	(SEGOVIA *and* ESCOVEDO *go out.*)
RODRIGO	I don't want to go back to Palos prison.
BERNO	Neither do I.
RASCON	Columbus has shown Quintero and myself that he must be obeyed.
QUINTERO	He's brought us over to the Santa Maria to be under his watch . . . because . . . because of what was SAID of us on board the Pinta.
RODRIGO	You're right, Rascon! This Admiral must be obeyed.
BERNO	I'll get to work.
	(BERNO *goes out and is followed by most of the* SAILORS.)
GRECO	(*calling after sailors*) Wait till you're too weak to work! (*to Carlo and Fernando*) They'll follow ME later – you'll see! Come on! (*They follow other sailors out.*)

★   ★   ★   ★   ★

(ESCOVEDO *walks across deck with Record Book.*)

ESCOVEDO   (*stopping to read*) 'SUNDAY, 9th SEPTEMBER – just three days out.' (*looking up*) I wonder what this day will bring? The crew are uneasy and quick to temper. (*sniffing air*) I smell trouble! (*He goes out.*)

(RASCON *and* QUINTERO *run onto deck.*)

RASCON   It wasn't my fault! I held the wheel steady!

QUINTERO   The needle fell away to the north-east before my eyes.

RASCON   (*rubbing head and ears*) That Alonzo is a brute! It was an ill day for us when we were put aboard this ship, Quintero.

QUINTERO   (*rubbing shoulders*) What fools we were to hole the Pinta's . . . (*As he speaks,* DOMINO *comes in.*)

DOMINO   You did it then?

(RASCON *holds Domino, putting hand over his mouth, while* QUINTERO *threatens him with knife.*)

RASCON   Did what? What did you hear, boy?

DOMINO   (*choking*) I . . . I . . . I . . .

QUINTERO   Will you hold your tongue? Or shall I cut it out for safety?

DOMINO   (*screaming*) No! No! No!

(BERNO *and* RODRIGO *rush in and pull Domino free.*)

BERNO   (*to Rascon*) Leave the boy!

RODRIGO   (*to Quintero*) What has he done? (*to Domino*) What have you done, boy?

RASCON   (*threateningly to Domino*) Speak up, boy! What did you hear?

16

DOMINO	Nothing . . . I heard nothing! (*He runs out.*)
QUINTERO	That's well!
	(GRECO, CARLO *and* FERNANDO *come in, followed by* ALONZO.)
ALONZO	You stupid, ignorant fools!
GRECO	The needle fell to the north-east before my eyes, Master Pilot.
ALONZO	You let it slip – as did these two.
CARLO	No, Master Pilot!
FERNANDO	We held the needle with all our strength.
ALONZO	(*angrily*) Weaklings! Am I to pilot this ship to India with a crew of ignorant weaklings?
	(COLUMBUS *strides in.*)
COLUMBUS	What is all this, Alonzo?
ALONZO	These fools, my Lord Columbus – whom you call seamen – can't hold a ship's wheel steady.
COLUMBUS	(*holding up hand to Alonzo*) Peace, Master Pilot! (*to sailors*) Get to your work men, and do it well if you want rations.
	(SAILORS *hurry out.*)
ALONZO	It was a mistake to take on these gaol-birds, Admiral. They are too ignorant to keep a course – even when it is set.
COLUMBUS	We had no choice, Alonzo. So many seamen would not brave the unknown seas and come with us.
	(SEGOVIA *and* ESCOVEDO *come in.*)
SEGOVIA	What's troubling the crew, Admiral? We are only three days out to sea and already the men are restless and uneasy.
COLUMBUS	They're ignorant fellows, Master Segovia, and fear to travel the high seas without sight of land.

17

SEGOVIA	That looks bad. We are but three days out . . . some . . . how far, Escovedo?
ESCOVEDO	(*from Record Book*) 'We were becalmed on Friday and only sailed four leagues . . . Saturday nine leagues . . .'
SEGOVIA	The voyage has scarcely begun! We shall not see land for many days and nights.
COLUMBUS	And yet I'm told that, some twenty leagues to the west of the Canaries, islands are sighted in the mist from time to time.
ALONZO	I was told this too, by Spaniards living on the islands back in Gomera.
SEGOVIA	Islands in the mist! They could be phantom islands, my Lord Columbus!
ESCOVEDO	Phantoms!
ALONZO	(*laughing*) Don't breathe a word to the men of PHANTOM islands, Master Segovia. (*waving hand*) I'll to my work. (*He goes out.*)
SEGOVIA	Come, Escovedo – your records must be exact – and I have my accounts to check. (*They both go out.*)
COLUMBUS	(*taking Log Book from inside picket*) Exact, he says! This is the exact record of the voyage and it must NEVER leave my person, whether I sleep or wake. (*opening book*) 'Saturday I gave out 9 leagues sailed, when it was 12.' (*looking up*) Each day I'll do the same! None must know how far we are from land – none but myself.
VOICE OF SAILOR	WRECK AHOY! WRECK AHOY!
	(SAILORS *rush onto deck.*)
DOMINO	Master Columbus! Admiral! Did you hear?
COLUMBUS	Hear what?
VOICE OF SAILOR	WRECK AHOY!

SAILORS	(*disappointed*) WRECK! Only a WRECK!
DOMINO	Wreck! I thought it was LAND ahoy, I heard!
COLUMBUS	Men! Land WILL be seen, but NOT YET! (*He goes out.*)
GRECO	'Land will be seen,' he says, 'BUT NOT YET!' Not EVER, if you ask me!
CARLO	Why did we come? (*looking wildly round*) Why did we agree to come?
GRECO	We agreed to come because we were in that stinking Palos prison and we wanted our freedom.
FERNANDO	Aye! They got ME out of Palos prison, but where did they get this Christopher Columbus from?
GRECO	Out of the mad-house! (*He runs to side of ship.*) Look out there! (*All look out to sea.*) He's mad!
SAILORS	Mad! Mad! MAD!
GRECO	(*coming back*) Nothing but water! What will happen to us when we get to the edge?
RASCON	What edge? Columbus says the world's not flat.
QUINTERO	He says it's round.
GRECO	What does Columbus know about navigation? He's a map-maker. He hasn't sailed the high seas – except in his imagination and his books! (*turning to sailors and pointing towards sea*) The world – out there – is FLAT! It's as flat as a pancake and Columbus is a mad-man! You'll remember my words! You'll see!
BERNO	(*rushing to side and pointing to sky*) Look!
RODRIGO	(*following*) What do you see, Berno?
DOMINO	(*following*) It's a bird! (*disappointed*) It's just a bird!
BERNO	It's a *land* bird!
	(ALL *rush to side and look out.*)

RODRIGO	A wagtail – and there are some more down there, sleeping and riding on the water.
BERNO	These wagtails are never to be found more than 20 leagues from land.
RODRIGO	You're right, Berno. We'll get to work.
	(RODRIGO *moves out and is followed by most of the* SAILORS.)
GRECO	(*calling after sailors*) Wait till you're too weak to work! (*to* CARLO *and* FERNANDO) You stick with me! (*They follow sailors out.*)

★   ★   ★   ★   ★

(ESCOVEDO *walks across deck with Record Book.*)

ESCOVEDO	(*stopping to read*) 'WEDNESDAY, 19th SEPTEMBER . . . thirteen days out . . .' (*looking up*) And by my reckoning we have sailed 440 leagues. (*He goes out.*)

(COLUMBUS *walks across deck.* DOMINO *runs after him with papers.*)

DOMINO	My Lord Admiral! Here are messages . . . come over on the ship's line from the captains of Pinta and Nina.
COLUMBUS	(*taking papers*) Give them to me, boy! Ah! By Captain Pinzon's reckoning we have sailed some 440 leagues, but . . . Captain Yanez makes it less . . . he says 420. (*louder*) The captains don't agree! (*smiling*) None of us do!

(GRECO *comes in and slips quietly up behind Columbus.*)

GRECO	Why is that, Admiral? Why don't you all agree?
COLUMBUS	(*firmly*) The instruments on Pinta and Nina play false – but ours, on the flagship, are true. I'll go and measure the true distance. (*He calls back as he goes out.*) But we must be half-way!

(*Enter* CARLO *and* FERNANDO.)

CARLO Half-way? Half-way to what?

FERNANDO Greco! Talk to the others! They will follow you. (*to Domino*) Clear off, Long Ears!

DOMINO Last night I thought my ears heard nightingales sing. Admiral Columbus thought he heard them too.

OTHERS Nightingales!

GRECO (*scoffing*) More like mocking birds!

OTHERS (*echoing*) Mocking birds!

DOMINO (*pointing*) They're still out there, floating on the weeds. Berno says that they're wagtails and are never to be found more than 20 leagues from land.

GRECO (*scoffing*) Wagtails . . . (*going to side and looking out*) weeds! I don't like these weeds. (*looking up*) The ship's not moving!

CARLO (*yells*) Why don't we move?

FERNANDO There's no wind, Carlo! No wind at all.

(*Other* SAILORS *come in.*)

BERNO That's right – we're becalmed!

RODRIGO We don't move in any direction.

GRECO So we couldn't return to Spain now, even if Admiral Columbus gave the order.

BERNO So we must go ON, Greco, perhaps who knows – to riches!

RODRIGO Remember that, comrades! When we do return to Spain, we'll be rich.

(COLUMBUS *strides in, carrying papers.*)

COLUMBUS You WILL be rich, men! And your families will greet you all with open arms.

21

GRECO	(*pointing out to sea*) Well, we can't spend our money here, Admiral! You've brought us to a sea of weeds.
COLUMBUS	(*opening papers*) These charts have just come over on the line from Pinta and Nina.
	(SAILORS *gather round Columbus.*)
	Come and look. We're here!
BERNO	What are these marks, Admiral?
COLUMBUS	According to Captain Pinzon . . . these ahead of us . . . are . . . islands.
SAILORS	Islands!
COLUMBUS	We'll look at Captain Yanez' chart.
BERNO	Look! The Captain of Nina has marked in the islands too!
GRECO	(*grabbing charts*) But they're not in the same place!
COLUMBUS	(*taking charts*) These charts are being drawn up for the first time! How can they be exact? (*to Berno*) Give me the astrolabe.
VOICE OF PINZON	COLUMBUS! AHOY! WE MOVE!
SAILORS	Pinzon's voice!
COLUMBUS	He's hailing from the Pinta. (*holding up hand*) Peace!
VOICE OF PINZON	COLUMBUS! LAND AHOY!
SAILORS	LAND! LAND!
COLUMBUS	I'll go up to the poop deck!
	(COLUMBUS *hurries out, followed by* DOMINO. SAILORS *rush to side of ship and look out.*)
BERNO	We're only some twenty days out from Gomera. Can we have reached the Indies?

RODRIGO	If so . . . the Earth must be a globe. (*to Greco*) And Columbus is right.
BERNO	And Captain Pinzon will have won the prize!
RASCON	What prize?
RODRIGO	The King's prize, Rascon. King Ferdinand promised a fortune to the first man to sight the Indies.

(*Enter* SEGOVIA *and* ESCOVEDO.)

QUINTERO	(*excitedly*) Captain Pinzon has sighted land, my Lords!
RASCON	So Captain Pinzon wins the King's prize.
QUINTERO	How much is it? Tell us, Master Escovedo.
ESCOVEDO	(*from book*) 'The King has offered 10,000 maradevis . . . A YEAR, to the first man to sight the Indies.'
SAILORS	(*to each other*) A YEAR!
SEGOVIA	The paying of this money will be subject to MY ruling. Remember – I am the King's eyes upon this voyage.
RASCON	Look out to the west, Master Segovia, and see it for yourself.
SEGOVIA	(*walking to side*) I can see nothing!
ESCOVEDO	(*following*) Nor I!
RASCON	Climb up . . .
QUINTERO	. . . and skin your eyes. (*They mime pushing Segovia overboard behind his back.*)
RASCON	Listen!
QUINTERO	They're singing the Gloria, aboard the Pinta!
DISTANT VOICES	Gloria! Gloria! Gloria in excelcis Deo!

SAILORS   (*falling to knees*)
Gloria! Gloria!
Gloria in excelcis Deo.

(ALONZO *strides in.*)

ALONZO   The Admiral Columbus has changed our course.
We're to sail south-west towards the islands
sighted by Captain Pinzon.

GRECO   I don't believe it!

(ALL *turn towards Greco in surprise.*)

A while back Columbus was saying that we were
half-way. We've come only a few leagues since.

BERNO   But we heard the Gloria!

RODRIGO   There will be islands in the seas – out from the
Indies. (*to Segovia*) You're a learned man, Master
Segovia. What do you think?

SEGOVIA   I think the King's reward is still there for all to
strive for!

ESCOVEDO   (*gloomily*) I saw nothing!

ALONZO   Take heart! Some islands HAVE been sighted.
We all heard the voice of Pinta's Captain. (*putting
up hand*) The wind blows fair! I'll to the
bridge – so get about your work.

(ALONZO *goes out one way,* BERNO *and* RODRIGO
another.)

GRECO   'Get to your work!' he says. I want more than
work. I want riches.

(CARLO *and* FERNANDO *nod in agreement.*)

SEGOVIA   All the riches you'll get for the next few weeks
will be your daily rations.

GRECO   (*angrily*) They're not enough!

SEGOVIA	They're the best rations ever given out to seamen. (*taking book from Escovedo*) 'One libra of meat, one libra of ship's biscuits, half a quarto of wine . . . and portions of cheese, onions and vinegar to keep you healthy.' Count yourselves lucky! (*He goes out, followed by* ESCOVEDO.)
RASCON	It's true. The rations are good!
QUINTERO	Better than in Palos prison. (*They go out.*)
GRECO	They're still loyal – even those two! Never fear, comrades! My turn will come! (*He goes out, followed by* CARLO *and* FERNANDO.)

★   ★   ★   ★   ★

(ESCOVEDO *walks across deck with Record Book.*)

ESCOVEDO	(*stopping to read*) 'THURSDAY, 11th OCTOBER . . . We are now some thirty-five days out and still no land.' (*He looks out to sea and sighs.*) The sea is less salt, they say . . . BUT WE DON'T SEE LAND! (*He walks off.*)

(COLUMBUS *walks slowly across deck.*)

COLUMBUS	(*taking Log Book from inside pocket*) 'DAY 35 . . . yesterday another 20 leagues, which I will call 16.' (*looking up*) The good Captain Pinzon is puzzled by the way the compass swings – and so am I! I sometimes feel that the Pole Star moves!

(ALONZO *walks in and stands still as Columbus turns.*)

	Ho there, Master Pilot! (*He puts Log Book in pocket.*)
ALONZO	Ho there, Admiral!
COLUMBUS	Something is troubling you, Alonzo! What is it?
ALONZO	(*taking a deep breath*) The charts, Admiral! The charts do not read true.

COLUMBUS	(*shrugging shoulders*) The compass swings about in a strange way. We are all puzzled – but we've already talked about this!
ALONZO	(*firmly*) Not the compass reading, Admiral. It's the distance we have travelled. (*taking Ship's Log from pocket*) Yesterday . . . Day 34 . . . it is written here we made but 16 leagues, but I'd swear on God's Holy Book, that it was 22.
COLUMBUS	Twenty-two! No! (*shaking head*) It could not be so far.
ALONZO	The charts sent over from the other ships give 21 and 22 leagues for yesterday. Why should Captain Pinzon's word not be as true as . . .
COLUMBUS	(*quietly*) Go on, Alonzo! Finish what you have to say.
ALONZO	My Lord . . . I'm troubled . . . by the way things are! The crew are restless and there is much talk of going back while we still live.
COLUMBUS	Is that all?
ALONZO	No that is not all, Columbus. There is talk of MUTINY!
COLUMBUS	That would be led by Greco!
ALONZO	You know then?
COLUMBUS	(*angrily*) Do you think I go about my business with shut eyes and ears? Call the men on deck.
ALONZO	(*warningly*) It may not be wise to call them all together.
COLUMBUS	So! (*He walks to side and calls.*) HO, THERE! HO! ALL MEN ON DECK!
ALONZO	Admiral! I must warn you! Their mood is dangerous.
	(SAILORS *hurry on deck.* SEGOVIA *and* ESCOVEDO *follow and stand apart.*)

COLUMBUS	(*to muttering sailors*) Captain Alonzo tells me you are troubled.
SAILORS	(*surging forward as muttering grows louder*) Aye! Aye! We're troubled!
GRECO	More than troubled, Admiral!
COLUMBUS	(*holding up hand*) Wait, Greco! Let me speak.
GRECO	(*as muttering grows even louder*) Give him this chance, men. Let him speak. (*muttering quietens*)
COLUMBUS	Men! My plan is to sail on for TWO more days. When those two days are up, we'll meet here on this deck. Then you shall tell me what you want to do.
GRECO	You mean you'll turn back, Admiral?
COLUMBUS	I mean, I'll listen to you! NOW! (*looking slowly at each sailor*) THROW YOUR WEAPONS DOWN UPON THE DECK! Greco! You first! I know you have a knife. (GRECO *throws down knife.*) And now your other one! (GRECO *reluctantly throws down second knife.*) Rascon! (RASCON *throws down knife.*) And now the rest of you! (*Others throw down knives.*) In TWO DAYS, then! You have my word!
	(DOMINO *runs in, carrying a branch of roseberries.*)
DOMINO	Look! A tree branch . . . bearing green leaves and rosy berries.
COLUMBUS	(*fingering branch*) This is a fresh branch! (*smiles*) We may not need TWO DAYS!
BERNO	You may yet win the King's prize, Domino!
COLUMBUS	And to the King's prize I'll add my own reward.
DOMINO	What's that, my Lord?
COLUMBUS	A doublet of the finest silk . . . to wear when next you strut the streets of Palos.

(BERNO *and* RODRIGO *run out.*)

RASCON   (*to Greco*) I can see you now, Greco, as fine as any peacock!

QUINTERO   You may win the prize yourself, Rascon!

COLUMBUS   Any one of you can win. Come! Every man to the watch!

(SAILORS *run off, leaving* COLUMBUS, ALONZO, SEGOVIA, ESCOVEDO *and* DOMINO.)

ALONZO   (*bowing to Columbus*) You did well, my Lord Admiral. The men's mood has changed.

SEGOVIA   Let us hope it will not change back again too soon. I do not trust these seamen . . . they are bought too easily!

(BERNO *runs in.*)

BERNO   (*breathlessly*) Lord Admiral! Rodrigo has seen a light!

COLUMBUS   Where is it? Which direction?

BERNO   It's due west, my Lord.

ALONZO   What kind of light?

BERNO   I don't know. I didn't see it, but Rodrigo called down from the crow's nest.

ALONZO   What were his words, Berno?

BERNO   He called, 'A light – due west . . . a little light!' I did not tell the others.

(DOMINO *runs out.*)

COLUMBUS   That was wise, good Berno. After so many disappointments, we must be sure.

(RODRIGO *runs in.*)

RODRIGO   (*breathlessly*) My Lords! I've seen a flickering light out there towards the west.

ALONZO   What is it like?

RODRIGO	Like a wax candle . . . but it goes up and down . . . perhaps it is a fire.
COLUMBUS	Are you sure, Rodrigo?
RODRIGO	(*pointing to eyes*) I saw it with both these eyes.
COLUMBUS	I'll see it for myself. (*He hurries out.*)
	(RASCON *and* QUINTERO *run in, followed by* SAILORS)
RASCON	Where is the light? Where is it?
ALONZO	So! The news is out! Rodrigo saw it from the crow's nest.
	(SAILORS *run to side and look out, followed by* ALONZO.)
QUINTERO	I see it . . . no, I do not . . . I DO! It's there!
RODRIGO	(*triumphantly*) I saw it first. The silk doublet will be mine. (*He struts about.*)
VOICE OF COLUMBUS	HOVE TO! HOVE TO, I SAY! LAND AHOY!
ALONZO	Praise be to God! That was the Admiral's voice!
RASCON	It's the first time Columbus has called, 'Land Ahoy!'
QUINTERO	Then we HAVE reached the Indies!
	(*Enter* COLUMBUS.)
COLUMBUS	(*triumphantly*) LAND AHOY!
ALONZO	We heard you, Admiral!
COLUMBUS	Our faith is justified. We have reached the Indies! Thanks be to God!
ALL	THANKS BE TO GOD!
	(*They all go out repeating,* 'Thanks be to God!')

END OF FIRST PLAY

PLAYWATCHERS

Spanish Monks

FRANCISCO   So Columbus was right! (*spinning globe*) And yet he didn't know that he was only half-way to the East.

PAULO   His India was our West Indies!

BARTHOLOMEW   (*turning globe*) But he did enough to convince people that the Earth is shaped like this.

FRANCISCO   (*thoughtfully*) To go out as he did . . . and then to return safely . . . made all the difference to those who followed him.

PAULO   To go first . . . that makes him the greatest explorer of them all.

FRANCISCO   All great explorers play their part. (*picking up another book*) You must turn your attention to this book next, Bartholomew.

BARTHOLOMEW   (*reads*) 'The Journal of Vasco da Gama, Admiral and Lord of Portugal.'

PAULO   Print this journal next, Bartholomew.

FRANCISCO   (*opening book*) JULY 1497 (*reads*) 'Left Portugal on board my flagship, Santa Gabriel . . .'

BARTHOLOMEW   (*reading on*) '. . . following the route of Admiral Diaz.'

PAULO   Ah! So da Gama was not sailing into unknown seas!

BARTHOLOMEW	Look in here! He admits he hugged the coast of Africa.
PAULO	And then he lost his way! Da Gama always needed pilots. Columbus was the greater . . .
FRANCISCO	(*holding up hand*) You are too hasty, Brother Paulo! Read on and you will see just what da Gama did.
PAULO	Brother Francisco! Let's make another voyage . . . in our imagination . . . and from the safety of our library.

Here begins the story of Vasco da Gama

Vasco da Gama

Playmakers

The officers

VASCO DA GAMA – Admiral on the flagship, Santa Gabriel
BRAGANZA – Pilot of Santa Gabriel
CASTRO ⎫
PEREZ ⎭ Navigators of Santa Gabriel

MASTER PADRO – Recorder of the voyage
FATHER DOM ANTONIO – a priest

The crew

LOPEZ   ⎫
ZARCO   ⎬ hard-working seamen
PERESTELLO ⎭

INEZ ⎫
DIEGO ⎭ seamen who cause trouble

Ship's boy
Other seamen

Foreign pilots

SAUD   ⎫ Arab pilots who are forced to act as pilots between
MUSTAPHA ⎭ Mozambique and Malindi

IBN MADJID – a Master Astrologer pilot who acts as pilot between
Malindi and Calicut

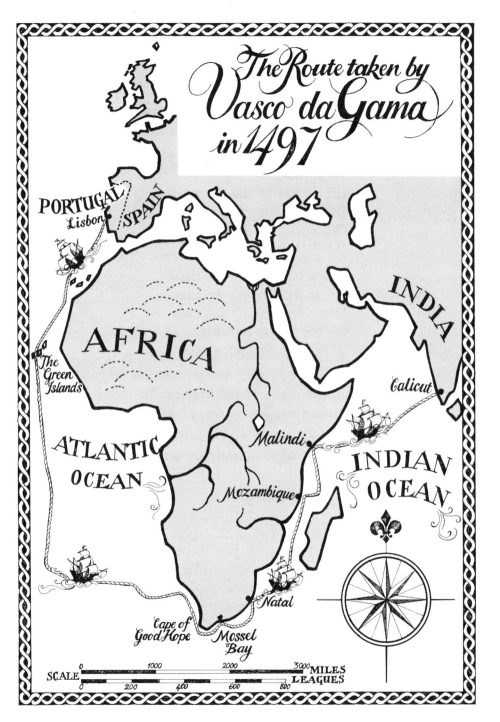

33

Vasco da Gama

LOPEZ, ZARCO, PERESTELLO *and other* SEAMEN *struggle across the deck of the Santa Gabriel, carrying stores.* MASTER PADRO *strides about, 'marking off' the stores in his book.*

SAILORS   (*sing, see p.77 for music, laughing and miming throughout*)
Off we sail on the Santa Gabriel,
Off we sail on the Santa Gabriel,
Off we sail on the Santa Gabriel
On the way to fortune!

Heave-ho! And up she rises!
Heave-ho! And up she rises!
Heave-ho! And up she rises
On the way to fortune!

PADRO   (*reading from book*) 'MONDAY 8th JULY, YEAR 1497 . . . 20 guns and powder . . . 40 good cross-bows . . . hand-weapons for each man . . .' (*looking up*) So . . . we're ready to sail!

LOPEZ   (*looking over Padro's shoulder*) The rations, Master Padro? What are the crew's rations for the voyage?

SAILORS   Aye! The rations!

(SAILORS *stop work and crowd round.*)

PADRO   (*reads*) 'For each man the daily ration shall be . . .
Ship's biscuits—one and a half libras,
Water—one quarto,
Wine—half of one quarto,
Some oil and vinegar . . .'

LOPEZ   What of the meat?

SAILORS   Aye! The meat!

PADRO   (*reads*) 'DRIED SALT FISH . . .'

LOPEZ	But . . . the meat?
PADRO	It's written down here . . . 'GOAT'S FLESH . . . (*groans*) . . . and GOOD BEEF OF PORTUGAL . . .'
SAILORS	(*cheering*) BEEF!
LOPEZ	How much? What's the ration of beef for each man, each day?
PADRO	(*reads*) 'One whole libra.' Seamen have never had so much beef before.
ZARCO	Seamen have never set out on such a voyage before, Master Padro.
PERESTELLO	Tell the Admiral we'll eat the goat's flesh on our way home again – when we return!
LOPEZ	Then we can mix it with the SPICES that we get from India.
ZARCO	We'll be content to suffer a little on our way home . . .
PERESTELLO	. . . when our pockets are lined with Eastern treasure.
VOICE OFF	WE SAIL! ANCHORS AWAY!
	(SAILORS *run across deck with ropes, and all on board mime movements of moving ship.*)
SAILORS	(*sing, laughing and miming throughout*) Off we sail on the Santa Gabriel, Off we sail on the Santa Gabriel, Off we sail on the Santa Gabriel On the way to fortune!
	Heave-ho! And up she rises! Heave-ho! And up she rises! Heave-ho! And up she rises On the way to fortune!
	(SAILORS *run to side of ship away from audience and wave 'goodbyes'.*)

35

PADRO (*closing book*) So . . . the voyage begins. The sailors are in good heart. Let's hope they stay cheerful all the way. (*He goes out.*)

(DA GAMA *strides onto the deck, followed by* FATHER DOM ANTONIO *and* SHIP'S BOY, *carrying holy flag.*)

DA GAMA Ho there! (SAILORS *turn round and run forward.*) So . . . you are already idle!

LOPEZ (*nervously*) We wave goodbye to Portugal, Lord Admiral, . . . that's all.

(ZARCO *runs forward and kneels before flag as* SAILORS *move back.*)

ZARCO (*to Dom Antonio*) We beg you, good Father Antonio, to bless the Santa Gabriel . . .

PERESTELLO . . . and all who sail in her.

DOM ANTONIO (*holding up hand*) God speed, good ship! (*making sign of cross*) May the good Lord go with us on our voyage.

SAILORS (*all on one knee*) May the good Lord go with us on our voyage.

DOM ANTONIO Be of good courage! The Lord is with you.

DA GAMA (*impatiently*) Enough! We said our prayers last night in the Chapel of the blessed Knights of Christ. The voyage is *already* blessed. (*waving arm*) Get to your work!

(SAILORS *hurry out, followed by* DOM ANTONIO *and* SHIP'S BOY *with flag.*)

Where's my pilot? Ho there, Braganza!

(CASTRO *and* PEREZ, *the two navigators, hurry in.*)

CASTRO Braganza is up there . . . (*pointing*) . . . on the poop deck . . .

PEREZ . . . checking his compass.

DA GAMA	There's no need for Braganza to pilot us out of home waters. Admiral Diaz is out there (*pointing*) . . . ahead of us.
CASTRO	How far is Diaz to pilot us, Lord Admiral?
DA GAMA	To the Green Islands. That will be far enough and then we'll make our own way. (*shouts*) Braganza!

(BRAGANZA *hurries in.*)

BRAGANZA	I've checked all the instruments, Lord Admiral. My compass is set square and true.
DA GAMA	(*impatiently*) We're making very little sail. We must get on, Braganza! Diaz is way ahead and we must use him as our pilot to the Green Islands.
BRAGANZA	(*angrily*) There was no need to have the Admiral Diaz to pilot us. I know the way.
DA GAMA	What's our speed? We're hardly moving!
BRAGANZA	(*sulkily*) There is no wind! I can't help that!
PEREZ	Easy now, Braganza! (*looking up*) The air's too still. If this mist rises any more, we shall have to make our own way.
CASTRO	(*looking up*) No sun! I can't check my astrolabe without sun.
VOICE OFF	FOG AHOY! PILOT!
BRAGANZA	Fog! You're right, Perez. This fog means that we shall soon lose Diaz.

(BRAGANZA *hurries out as* SHIP'S BOY *runs in.*)

SHIP'S BOY	My Lord da Gama! You're wanted!
DA GAMA	Where and what for? I'm not at everyone's beck and call!
SHIP'S BOY	Inez and Diego . . . in the hold . . . they're fighting . . . there's blood everywhere.

DA GAMA (*angrily*) There'll be more blood when I have done! I'll flog the pair of them myself!

(DA GAMA *strides out followed by* SHIP'S BOY.)

CASTRO (*mournfully*) The signs are not good, Perez!

PEREZ Well . . . (*laughing*) not for Inez and Diego! But they must be taught a lesson. Da Gama is quite right to be firm from the start.

CASTRO Agreed! (*taking out chart*) Look at this chart again. It's a three-months-long sail to the . . . Cape of Storms.

PEREZ Don't call it that! The King has ordered that the Cape of Storms must be renamed, Cape of Good Hope.

CASTRO (*sighing*) Three months . . . or more . . . before we reach . . . GOOD HOPE!

PEREZ Take heart! Think of our ships . . . they're sound . . . the very best and built for the purpose. Look out there! Look through the fog! You see . . . they ride the waves like ducks!

CASTRO True! But you must agree, Perez, that there's nothing but sea and sky out there. (*pointing*) It's empty!

PEREZ Empty! (*laughing*) I'm empty! (*He pats his stomach.*) We'll fill ourselves. Come on! (*They go out.*)

    ★   ★   ★   ★   ★

(PADRO *walks across deck with the Ship's Log.*)

PADRO (*opening book*) '1st MARCH 1498 . . . the eighth month since we left Spain . . .' (*looking up*) And still we seem as far away from India as ever.

(*Enter* DOM ANTONIO.)

Greetings, good Father! (*He sighs and closes the book.*)

DOM ANTONIO	What's the matter Padro?
PADRO	We've sailed these dreary seas for eight long months – and still – NO INDIA.
	(*Enter* CASTRO *and* PEREZ.)
CASTRO	Eight months is it, Padro? It seems more like eight years since we left home.
PEREZ	(*regretfully*) And we thought we'd all be rich by now!
DOM ANTONIO	We came to spread the news of Jesus Christ among the heathen peoples too – don't forget that!
PADRO	(*smiling*) Good Father! You may have come to spread God's word, but I don't think many of our crew set out as missionaries of Christ!
CASTRO	Can you imagine Inez and Diego as peacemakers?
PEREZ	(*miming*) Peace be unto you, good people!
	(CASTRO *and* PEREZ *mime a fight. All laugh.*)
DOM ANTONIO	Good! You laugh! We must all keep our spirits up.
PADRO	Even da Gama loses heart at times. (*opening Ship's Log*) It's written here in his own hand – '22nd SEPTEMBER . . . nothing but a lonely, dreary waste of seas and endless skies.'
CASTRO	That was written when we . . . (*sighing*) sailed too far to the west. That was my mistake.
PEREZ	The currents were not charted on Diaz' old map.
DOM ANTONIO	But remember the good times we had. Remember the feasting in Mossel Bay!
CASTRO	When da Gama traded one small round bell, three tin rings and a bracelet . . .
PEREZ	. . . for a fat ox!
ALL	(*rubbing stomachs*) Ah! It was good!

39

PADRO	And then on December 25th . . . (*reads*) 'God in His Mercy has allowed us to see land on Christmas Day, which we shall call, NATAL.'
DOM ANTONIO	God in His mercy, and I in mine! Those villains, Inez and Diego must be brought up on deck to breathe some of God's good air – or we shall be saying prayers for corpses! (*smiling*) I'll see to it.
PADRO	You've done much to keep our spirits up, Father Antonio. I'll go with you. (*They both go out.*)
CASTRO	Too many of the crew are sick. We must find an anchorage and take in fresh water and supplies.
PEREZ	(*rubbing mouth*) This scurvy is a horrible disease. (*rubbing gums*) I lost two teeth last night. Look!
CASTRO	My gums are raw and bleeding!
	(BRAGANZA *comes in.*)
BRAGANZA	Shut up your trap-doors! The scurvy rots us all. (*sitting on barrel*) I'm exhausted!
CASTRO	How is the Admiral? What's his temper like today, Braganza?
BRAGANZA	Terrible! But his will is iron! (*putting head into hands*)
PEREZ	We'll do a watch and give you some relief.
	(CASTRO *and* PEREZ *hurry out.*)
BRAGANZA	(*calling after them*) The Admiral's up there too! (*looking round*) I'll find a quiet place . . . (*Loud voices are heard.*) No peace! (*He groans and lies down at side of deck.*)
	(INEZ *and* DIEGO *stagger on deck, stretching their limbs.*)
INEZ	(*gulping*) Give me some air! (*clasping head*) My head is spinning round.
DIEGO	And mine! (*sitting on barrel*) Look at my arms and legs! I'm nothing but skin and bones.

INEZ	(*spitting onto hand*) And I'm spitting blood again! My mouth is rotting from this filthy water.
DIEGO	(*dropping voice*) Da Gama has brought us all to this!
INEZ	The brute!
DIEGO	Never did men have such a man of iron to lead them. (*He rubs his shoulders.*)
INEZ	I've still got the scars from the flogging he gave us. And now he keeps us penned below like animals.
DIEGO	(*staggering to his feet*) Aye! Like animals! If da Gama were here, I'd tell him . . .
INEZ	(*in horror*) Tell him! Tell him what, Diego?
DIEGO	I'D . . . TELL . . . HIM . . .

(DA GAMA *strides in.*)

DA GAMA	Who would you tell, Diego? And what would you say?

(INEZ *and* DIEGO *cower back and then move forward.*)

INEZ	My Lord Admiral . . . have some mercy! We need fresh water . . . and fresh air!
DIEGO	Give us the chance to work . . . up here on deck!
DA GAMA	(*thoughtfully*) Now could be the time to show a little mercy. (*to men*) Get forward and bring down the sail. I'll watch you!

(BRAGANZA *moves forward as* INEZ *and* DIEGO *hurry out.*)

BRAGANZA	Watch them, my Lord Admiral! Inez and Diego change direction more often than the wind.
DA GAMA	They know my strength! But from now on, Braganza, we need no enemies on board. Soon we shall have new enemies . . . (*pointing*) out there!

BRAGANZA	(*quickly*) Where are we then?
DA GAMA	(*taking chart from pocket*) Off an island they call Mozambique. The Sultan who rules there may well be friendly, but out in those waters . . . are the ARABS!
BRAGANZA	Arab traders! They won't be pleased to see us here.
DA GAMA	They'll be jealous of their trade. They'll want to keep it for themselves.
VOICE	**LAND AHOY! LAND AHOY!**
	(*All* SAILORS *rush in, followed by* PADRO, DOM ANTONIO *and* SHIP'S BOY.)
LOPEZ	Perez has sighted land, my Lord Admiral. I heard his call.
BRAGANZA	So did we all, you fool. We are not deaf.
ZARCO	(*to da Gama*) You'll anchor here awhile . . . and take on fresh water . . . won't you, my Lord?
PERESTELLO	Fresh water . . . and fresh meat?
DA GAMA	(*sighing*) They think of nothing but their bellies! (*turning to sailors*) Listen men! We will take on fresh supplies . . . but there is something more . . .
SAILORS	(*looking at each other*) What is it?
DA GAMA	This coast is unknown to us, but one thing is certain. (*pointing*) We shall find new enemies out there . . . ARABS!
SAILORS	(*in surprise*) Arabs!
SHIP'S BOY	What will Arabs want from us, Lord Admiral?
DA GAMA	Nothing FROM us. But they'll be afraid we'll take their trade. So skin your eyes and watch for Arab ships!

(SAILORS *move to side.* DA GAMA *and* BRAGANZA *study chart.*)

PADRO　　　　(*to Dom Antonio*) These Arabs will follow the Muslim faith.

DOM ANTONIO　That's so! (*laughing*) Are you thinking of preaching Christianity to them, Padro?

PADRO　　　　No! But if the Arabs have been trading among these islands, the native people may well be Muslims too.

DOM ANTONIO　In that case, we may well have enemies on both sea and land.

DA GAMA　　　(*looking up from chart*) We must have pilots from Mozambique to guide us north along this unknown coast.

BRAGANZA　　NATIVE pilots! But will they agree to come with us?

PADRO　　　　If the native people know the Arabs, they'll think of us as enemies.

DA GAMA　　　(*firmly*) They can be bought!

BRAGANZA　　(*in horror*) PILOT SLAVES! But they would harm our ships!

DA GAMA　　　Not slaves, Braganza! I mean to buy the services of native pilots with GOLD PIECES!

DOM ANTONIO　But what shall we do with these native pilots after they've shown the way?

DA GAMA　　　(*thoughtfully*) I shall offer each pilot thirty gold pieces and a promise to be put ashore . . . in one month's time. (*He goes out.*)

BRAGANZA　　(*doubtfully*) I hope the Admiral is right in this.

PADRO　　　　This could be our undoing!

DOM ANTONIO　Money . . . cannot buy loyalty!

*　　*　　*　　*　　*

(PADRO *walks across deck with the Ship's Log.*)

PADRO (*opening book*) 'TUESDAY 14th MARCH . . . We have put about some two weeks in these waters . . .' (*looking up*) That's in da Gama's hand. 'PUT ABOUT . . .' For two weeks we have sailed round in circles! (*He goes out.*)

(*Enter* CASTRO *and* PEREZ.)

CASTRO What else can you expect when da Gama takes such villains as Saud and Mustapha aboard as pilots?

PEREZ It would have been better to leave the piloting to Braganza.

(*Enter* BRAGANZA.)

BRAGANZA Da Gama won't do that! Don't you remember that he had Admiral Diaz to guide us from Portugal to the Green Islands – a route I've piloted a dozen times?

CASTRO But we lost Diaz in the fog, Braganza, and then you showed your skill.

PEREZ And if you're not up there . . . (*pointing at the wheel*) . . . you can't be blamed for our misfortunes. (*sighing*) I don't understand these currents . . . (*holding up hand*) and these strange winds.

BRAGANZA Take heart! We've covered a good distance since yesterday.

CASTRO Saud and Mustapha now know that they must take us to Malindi.

PEREZ A few words from da Gama . . . and a little boiling oil worked wonders!

BRAGANZA These Arab pilots know few of our words, but they understand us well enough.

CASTRO They understand da Gama!

PEREZ	They squealed like pigs when he dropped that oil upon their backs!
BRAGANZA	I wonder what else they know?
CASTRO	(*thoughtfully*) Let's have them here . . . and then find out.
BRAGANZA	Agreed! I'll put Lopez up there to hold the course. (*He hurries out.*)
PEREZ	(*anxiously*) This may not be wise. The Admiral . . .
CASTRO	The Admiral wants all the information he can get. But we'll let Braganza do it!
PEREZ	And then WE can't be blamed! Braganza shall be in charge of this.
	(BRAGANZA *comes in with the Arab pilots* SAUD *and* MUSTAPHA.)
CASTRO	We'll begin with signs of friendship. (*He mimes 'friendship'.*)
PEREZ	(*offering water-bag*) Drink! Drink! (*He mimes 'drink'.*)
	(SAUD *and* MUSTAPHA *look suspiciously at navigators.*)
BRAGANZA	(*taking water-bag*) I'll show them that it's not poisoned! (*He takes a drink.*) Good! (*He mimes 'good'.*)
SAUD	(*taking water-bag and drinking*) Good! Water . . . good!
MUSTAPHA	(*doing the same*) Good!
BRAGANZA	(*to Perez and Castro*) We want them to tell us how far it is to this place called Malindi . . .
CASTRO	. . . and how long they (*pointing to Saud and Mustapha*) . . . expect it to take . . .
PEREZ	. . . in a fair wind, such as we have now.

45

BRAGANZA	I'll try. (*to Saud and Mustapha*) MALINDI! (*He mimes 'understand?'*)
SAUD, MUSTAPHA	(*nodding*) MALINDI!
BRAGANZA	How far? (*holding up hand and counting fingers*) One! Two! Three! Four! Five! Six!
SAUD	(*looking puzzled and counting fingers*) One! Two! Three! Four! Five! Six!
MUSTAPHA	(*shaking head and opening arms wide*) No! No! (*closing hands close together*) ONE!
ALL PORTUGUESE	ONE . . . WHAT?
MUSTAPHA	(*pointing to sky as if to sun*) ONE!
BRAGANZA	I believe he means one DAY!
CASTRO	(*giving hour-glass to Saud*) Show! HOUR-GLASS!
SAUD	(*taking hour-glass and turning it up and down*) One! Two! Three! Four! Five! Six!
MUSTAPHA	SIX HOURS!
PEREZ	(*running to side of deck and looking out*) Can we be so near?
MUSTAPHA	(*blowing into air*) GOOD! GOOD!
BRAGANZA	WIND! (*blowing into air*) WIND!
SAUD	GOOD . . . WIND . . . SIX . . . HOURS!
	(BRAGANZA *and* CASTRO *happily slap each other on back.* SAUD *and* MUSTAPHA *run to side of deck.*)
MUSTAPHA	(*excitedly*) ZAVRA!
SAUD	Zavra! Zavra!
CASTRO	What is Zavra? (*He mimes 'what?'*)
MUSTAPHA	ZAVRA! (*He mimes 'man rowing boat'.*)
PEREZ	Fishing boats! Look! Zavra are fishing boats!
	(BRAGANZA *and* CASTRO *join others on the side.*)
BRAGANZA	We must be near . . .

VOICE OF LOPEZ	LAND AHOY! (*calls*) BRAGANZA!
	(BRAGANZA *rushes out.*)
CASTRO	(*excitedly to Saud and Mustapha*) What land is this? (*He mimes 'what?'*)
SAUD	MALINDI! (*pointing*) MALINDI!
PEREZ	(*suspiciously*) But they said six hours' sail away. It's more likely to be some little island. (*to Saud and Mustapha*) This . . . (*pointing*) not Malindi? (*He mimes 'doubt'.*)
MUSTAPHA	(*firmly*) MALINDI!
SAUD	MALINDI! (*Both mime 'definitely YES'.*)
	(DA GAMA *strides onto deck and looks round angrily.*)
DA GAMA	WHAT . . .!
CASTRO	(*excitedly*) My Lord Admiral! (*pointing*) The pilots say we've reached Malindi.
PEREZ	There are native rowing boats out there!
SAUD, MUSTAPHA	ZAVRA! (*They mime 'men rowing boats'.*)
DA GAMA	(*to Saud and Mustapha*) Get back up to Braganza!
	(*They hurry out.*)
	(*calls*) BRING DOWN THE SAILS!
	(PADRO *and* DOM ANTONIO *hurry in, followed by* SHIP'S BOY. SAILORS *run over deck.*)
	(*to navigators*) GET OUT YOUR CHARTS! Mark it all down!
DOM ANTONIO	The Lord be praised!
SHIP'S BOY	Amen to that!
PADRO	(*opening book*) Where are we now, Lord Admiral? What land is this?
DA GAMA	(*thoughtfully as he looks out*) We could be off . . . Malindi.

SAILORS	MALINDI!
PEREZ	My Lord Admiral! A short time ago the Arab pilots said Malindi was SIX HOURS' sail away . . .
DA GAMA	And you believed them! Those villains said six hours . . . AND YOU BELIEVED THEM! What fools you are!
CASTRO	What do you mean, Lord Admiral?
	(*Two loud splashes are heard.*)
VOICE OF BRAGANZA	MAN OVERBOARD! MAN OVERBOARD!
	(SAILORS *rush to side.*)
DA GAMA	(*sneering*) That's what I mean!
	(LOPEZ *runs in.*)
LOPEZ	My Lord Admiral! The Arab pilots have jumped overboard. (*He runs to side.*)
DOM ANTONIO	May God have mercy on their souls! (*He begins to make sign of cross.*)
DA GAMA	Save your prayers for Christian souls, Father Antonio! May those villains feed the fish! We have no use for them. I pray God the Malindi pilots will serve us better. (*He strides out.*)
PADRO	(*writing in book*) I shall record . . . 'two Arab pilots overboard as we approached Malindi . . .'
LOPEZ	(*calls over*) Those Arab pilots . . . Saud and Mustapha . . . are being picked up by natives in their fishing boats!
CASTRO	Fishing boats . . . ZAVRA! You remember how glad they were to see them.
PEREZ	(*regretfully*) Da Gama is right – AGAIN!
	(ALL *go out murmuring,* 'Da Gama is right!')

★   ★   ★   ★   ★

48

(PADRO *walks across deck with the Ship's Log.*)

PADRO   (*opening book*) 'SUNDAY 17th MAY in the year of the Lord 1498'. (*looking up*) We left Malindi just one month ago . . . (*from book*) '. . . with the King's blessing and his best pilot, a certain astronomer named Ibn Madjid. This pilot knows the route to Calicut well and is the best pilot I have ever known . . .' (*looking up*) Written in da Gama's hand! Mmm! 'The best pilot I have ever known . . .' But it has not made him popular! (*He goes out.*)

(BRAGANZA *comes in, throwing and catching a die in the air.*)

BRAGANZA   (*bitterly*) Whichever way it falls – I cannot win. (*sighing*) Only Ibn Madjid has da Gama's favour now.

(*Enter* CASTRO *and* PEREZ.)

CASTRO   You take it too hard, Braganza!

PEREZ   You did your part from the Green Islands to Mozambique.

BRAGANZA   But now I am forgotten. It's all . . . IBN MADJID . . . the MASTER pilot.

CASTRO   Braganza! You cannot know these currents and these winds as Madjid does.

PEREZ   And to be fair, you cannot fault the man's knowledge of the sea and sky. Last night I saw the North Star for the first time in months.

BRAGANZA   (*angrily*) I didn't lose the North Star from the sky! Psst! (*He spits.*) If I'm forgotten when fortunes are shared out . . . I'll split this Madjid's throat!

CASTRO   If you have any fortune left by then, Braganza! It's been put about that you're dicing with money you haven't got.

PEREZ   You'd be wiser not to play dice with Lopez and his friends, Braganza.

(CASTRO *and* PEREZ *go out, as* LOPEZ *and other* SAILORS *come in, all throwing and catching dice.*)

LOPEZ   Another game, Braganza? What shall we play for?

BRAGANZA   Nothing!

ZARCO   Nothing! Come on, Braganza! (*cunningly*) Today it's your turn to win.

BRAGANZA   (*bitterly*) It's never my turn to win these days. I win nothing but misfortune . . . (*half to himself*) since Madjid became the MASTER pilot of this ship. (*He goes out.*)

PERESTELLO   He takes it badly!

INEZ   (*laughing*) But we've taken plenty from him!

DIEGO   (*taking papers from pocket*) Which he must pay in gold when we return to Portugal.

INEZ   Braganaza hasn't got his fortune yet, Diego!

DIEGO   He'll pay . . . or . . . (*miming 'cutting throat'*) he'll pay that way!

LOPEZ   We shall all get our share. But da Gama stands to make a fortune! He'll be rich for ever.

ZARCO   It's said he'll get 400 times the buying price for ginger when he sells it at home in Portugal.

PERESTELLO   And more for cloves and pepper.

LOPEZ   There are other spices in India which they call CINN-A-MON and NUT-MEG. We shall all get our share of riches.

(SAILORS *mime 'pleasure in riches' as* IBN MADJID *comes in.*)

LOPEZ   Here comes the Master Pilot. (*He tosses dice in the air.*)

MADJID	(*slowly*) You play . . . DICE - yes?
ZARCO	We play dice! Yes!
MADJID	(*slowly*) I, Ibn Madjid . . . play dice - yes?
PERESTELLO	Not with us, you don't!
LOPEZ	(*hurriedly*) You are too good for us, Master pilot.
ZARCO	Besides, who steers the ship and watches the stars while you play dice?
MADJID	(*slowly*) The pilot . . . Braganza. He can do it.

(SAILORS *laugh.*)

LOPEZ	(*shaking head*) Oh no, Madjid! Braganza won't steer the ship. He is . . . not the pilot now.
MADJID	(*proudly*) That is so. The Admiral da Gama orders me, Ibn Madjid, to pilot from Malindi to Calicut. That is what I know.
LOPEZ	You know it well, Madjid - but Braganza - he is . . . (*miming 'not wanted'*) . . . not wanted. Braganza is (*miming 'angry'*) angry.
MADJID	(*thoughtfully*) Ah! I will . . . make (*He mimes 'peace'.*) with him.

(DA GAMA *strides in.*)

DA GAMA	Ho there, Master pilot! Who holds your course?
MADJID	(*bowing*) Castro and Perez, your navigators. But I will go.
DA GAMA	Wait! How far is it now to Calicut?
MADJID	Calicut . . . we see . . . one hour.
SAILORS	ONE HOUR!
DA GAMA	One hour! After so many months - only one hour! (*to sailors*) Ho there! Get to the rigging! Search the sea and sky. A marlota, a new suit of clothes, to the man who first sights India.

	(SAILORS *rush out excitedly*.)
MADJID	(*bowing to da Gama*) I go back to my place . . . (*thoughtfully*) and I will have Braganza with me, if he will come. (*He goes out.*)
DA GAMA	Ah! Braganza! We shall need him on our return! RETURN! We haven't got there yet! (*He walks slowly to the side.*) Could it be that I shall see India first? (*He looks out, rubbing his eyes.*) Out there are . . . pale blue peaks . . . or is it my imagination? My eyes have searched the sea so long . . .
VOICES OFF	LAND AHOY! LAND AHOY!
DA GAMA	(*sinking to knees and shouting*) Thanks be to Christ!
	(ALL *except Madjid hurry on deck. They stand still at the sight of da Gama on his knees.*)
CASTRO	Da Gama is thanking God!
PEREZ	Then we have reached Calicut and India! The Admiral would not be thanking the good Lord for yet more islands!
DOM ANTONIO	Thanks be to God!
ALL	Thanks be to God!
DA GAMA	(*walking forward and beckoning Padro*) Write it down . . . SUNDAY 17th MAY in the year 1498 . . . the Admiral da Gama sighted India. (*He turns to sailors and points out towards India.*) You'll find a thousand treasures there!
SAILORS	A THOUSAND TREASURES!
	(ALL *go out cheering and singing.*)

END OF SECOND PLAY

 **PLAYWATCHERS**

Spanish Monks

FRANCISCO	So . . . Columbus reached the WEST Indian islands, and then da Gama found India. First a Spaniard . . . and then a Portuguese! Mmm!
PAULO	Our two countries sit side by side upon the globe (*sighing*) but we are so jealous of each other.
BARTHOLOMEW	(*picking up book*) Then the story of this book will be the most extraordinary of all.
BOTH MONKS	What do you mean?
BARTHOLOMEW	(*turning globe*) Can you imagine it? The first voyage round the world under the command of a Portuguese Admiral with Spanish captains!
FRANCISCO	(*looking over Bartholomew's shoulder*) What's this? Ah! Pigafetta's Journal!
PAULO	(*excitedly*) PIGAFETTA! The noble Knight of Rhodes . . .
BARTHOLOMEW	. . . who wrote his story for the King of Spain, about Ferdinand Magellan.
FRANCISCO	Ferdinand Magellan! The one they called 'The Fox'.
BARTHOLOMEW	Just so! But Magellan, being Portuguese, needed all his cunning - to be Admiral of a SPANISH fleet.
PAULO	It couldn't work!
BARTHOLOMEW	(*laughing*) It didn't!

FRANCISCO The Spanish captains – did they . . . do for him?

BARTHOLOMEW Not so! He did for them – before they went far, too! But – let's go with him ourselves!

PAULO (*laughing*) Another voyage from our library! Which was Magellan's flagship?

BARTHOLOMEW (*turning pages*) That was the Trinidad – but we'll join . . . Vittoria – that was the only ship out of the five that set out, to come back here to Spain.

BOTH MONKS The Vittoria!

BARTHOLOMEW We'll join Vittoria!

Here begins the story of Ferdinand Magellan

Ferdinand Magellan

Playmakers

FERDINAND MAGELLAN – a Portuguese Admiral, known as 'The Fox'

HENRIQUE – Magellan's personal servant

MENDOZA
CARTEGENA
QUESADA
DE COCO
} the Spanish captains

ELCANO – a Spanish pilot

CAM
GASPAR
CABRAL
} Portuguese officers

BRUNO
RICARDO
RAPHAEL
} Portuguese seamen

Other seamen

PIGAFETTA – the Knight of Rhodes who recorded the voyage

The Route taken by Ferdinand Magellan in 1519

PACIFIC OCEAN

Islands of Thieves

The Philippines

Cebu

INDIAN OCEAN

AFRICA

SPAIN

ATLANTIC OCEAN

The Green Islands

SOUTH AMERICA

Patagonia

Straits of Magellan

PACIFIC OCEAN

SCALE

0   2000   4000   6000   8000 MILES
0   500 1000 1500 2000 2500 LEAGUES

Ferdinand Magellan

CAPTAIN MENDOZA *walks quickly onto the deck of the Vittoria,* *followed by* CARTEGENA *and* DE COCO.

MENDOZA   Wait! (*holding up hand*) The captains of the other ships have all rowed over. They'll meet us here on deck.

CARTEGENA   Not ALL the captains, Mendoza! (*laughing*) Not the captain of the flagship Trinidad! Not Ferdinand Magellan!

(ALL *spit.*)

DE COCO   The Admiral won't plot against himself!

(ALL *laugh nervously.*)

MENDOZA   The Fox of Portugal! Magellan is well named!

CARTEGENA   (*angrily*) How could the King of Spain . . . our King . . . give such a man charge over us?

DE COCO   My Spanish blood . . . (*taking dagger from robe*) boils over!

MENDOZA   For some five months now we've sailed the high seas, under the orders of this . . . foreign fox!

(ALL *spit.*)

CARTEGENA   And not once has he consulted us, or told us of his plans . . .

DE COCO   . . . or change of plans!

MENDOZA   So! Now we make our own! (*looking round*) Hist!

(CAPTAIN QUESADA *hurries in, followed by* ELCANO.)

Ho there, Quesada! Welcome! (*drawing back*) Why have you brought Elcano?

QUESADA   (*breathlessly*) I'll tell you . . .

CARTEGENA	Where's the captain of the San Antonio? (*suspiciously*) Where's Orago?
QUESADA	Dead!
ALL	DEAD!
MENDOZA	How?
QUESADA	Killed by my own hand! (*taking out bloody dagger*) This is Orago's blood!
DE COCO	(*in alarm*) Quesada! Where is the captain's body? Did you leave it on the San Antonio?

(ELCANO *moves forward and bows.*)

ELCANO	(*smirking*) Captain Orago feeds the fish! He's now a tasty morsel . . . for the sharks!
MENDOZA	(*to Quesada*) Tell us what happened.
QUESADA	It was as we planned. I went to Orago and told him that Magellan had disobeyed the King.
MENDOZA	What did he say to that?
QUESADA	Orago agreed that Magellan had not obeyed the King's instructions, to consult with us.
MENDOZA	But did he agree that this gave us a right to disobey Magellan?
QUESADA	(*shaking head*) No! He said that to disobey the Admiral on the high seas would be a mutiny.
MENDOZA	What then?
QUESADA	He talked of turning the San Antonio round and sailing her back home to Spain.
CARTEGENA	And then?
ELCANO	And then Quesada plunged his dagger into Orago's back!
MENDOZA	I'm uneasy – but we must go on with what we have resolved to do.

ALL	Agreed!
ELCANO	(*loudly*) Agreed!
DE COCO	(*suspiciously*) You agree too, Elcano? (*to others*) We don't know Elcano well enough to trust him.
	(ALL *look suspiciously at Elcano.*)
ELCANO	I'm your man!
QUESADA	(*to others*) It might be wiser to have him in it. He knows so much – and he saw me kill Orago!
MENDOZA	Can we trust you, Elcano?
ELCANO	I give you all my word!
MENDOZA	ON WHAT? (*Silence*) You're sharp witted and quick with your tongue, Elcano. What do you give your word on?
CARTEGENA	How can you give your word when you don't know our plan?
	(DE COCO *slips quietly behind Elcano and draws out his dagger.*)
ELCANO	You know I came here with Quesada. He had already told me you planned to . . . to . . . disobey the Admiral Magellan.
DE COCO	Or . . . TO MUTINY?
	(ELCANO *turns round quickly and sees dagger.*)
ELCANO	(*shouts*) NOT MUTINY! I did not say MUTINY!
	(MAGELLAN *rushes in, followed by* HENRIQUE, *who holds a dagger in each hand, and* PORTUGUESE OFFICERS *and* SEAMEN.)
MAGELLAN	So! My spies were right! IT'S MUTINY!
ALL PLOTTERS	NO! NO!
MAGELLAN	(*beckoning his men forward*) Hold them all!
	(MAGELLAN'S MEN *begin roping up plotters, except* ELCANO, *who breaks away.*)

ELCANO	Not me, Lord Admiral!
MAGELLAN	(*pulling out dagger*) Why not you, Elcano?
ELCANO	(*firmly*) You heard my words.
MAGELLAN	(*roughly*) But you are here, Elcano, so you're in it too!
ELCANO	You heard me say, 'NOT MUTINY'. You heard my words.
MAGELLAN	(*sneeringly*) But I don't know why you spoke them – or what was said before!
ELCANO	You saw that de Coco had his dagger ready to strike me down! (*He flings himself on one knee before Magellan.*) You saved my life, Lord Admiral!
MAGELLAN	Did I? And I'll take your life from you just as quickly if you ever play traitor to me. Remember that, Elcano! (*walking towards prisoners*) TRAITORS! (*taking letters from pocket*) Those letters which some of you sent by caravel, back to the King – I HAVE THEM HERE! (*He waves them in the plotters' faces.*)
MENDOZA	The letters which you have there, Magellan, are only of COMPLAINT against you.
CARTEGENA	There was no plan of mutiny.
DE COCO	We can all give our word on that!
MAGELLAN	You all give your words too easily! (*looking round*) You are all guilty of high treason . . .
ALL PLOTTERS	NO!
MAGELLAN	. . . because you planned to disobey the King's instructions . . . which were . . . (*shouts*) TO OBEY THE CAPTAIN GENERAL! (*pointing to himself*) WHICH . . . IS . . . ME! (*roughly*) Who is the ring-leader?

MENDOZA   (*stepping forward*) I wrote the letters, Admiral.

CARTEGENA   (*stepping forward*) And I stand beside Captain Mendoza.

MAGELLAN   (*sneeringly*) Then you can swing beside him from the yard-arm. (*to seamen*) Take them away!

(MENDOZA *and* CARTEGENA *are hustled out.*)

QUESADA   (*quietly*) Have you no mercy, Admiral?

MAGELLAN   For those who are against me . . . NO! You Spanish captains thought to bring me down, but I will not let you do it.

QUESADA   What is to be my fate?

MAGELLAN   (*cruelly*) We'll put you off along the coast . . . in Patagonia!

QUESADA   (*in horror*) Among the Giant People!

MAGELLAN   You'll have de Coco for company! (*to seamen*) Take them away!

(QUESADA *and* DE COCO *are hustled out.*)

MAGELLAN   (*thoughtfully*) Now I must find new captains – from the Portuguese who are loyal to me.

ELCANO   (*moving forward*) Admiral! I'm a pilot navigator – you know my skill!

MAGELLAN   I know your skill, Elcano. But can I be sure of you?

ELCANO   (*baring chest*) On my life, Admiral – I AM LOYAL!

MAGELLAN   (*beckoning Portuguese officers*) Cam! To the Concepcion!

CAM   At your will, Admiral! (*He hurries out.*)

MAGELLAN   Gaspar! The Santiago!

GASPAR   My Lord Admiral! (*He hurries out.*)

MAGELLAN	Cabral! The flagship! Take Trinidad!
CABRAL	At your command! (*He hurries out.*)
MAGELLAN	Elcano!
ELCANO	(*on one knee*) My Lord Admiral!
MAGELLAN	(*nodding*) You have more skill than all the others. Take Vittoria! Take this ship for your command.
ELCANO	(*bowing head*) I will serve you well, my Lord.
MAGELLAN	I will see you do! I'll be here with you!

(MAGELLAN *walks out.* HENRIQUE *motions to* ELCANO *to walk ahead and brings up the rear.*)

* * * * *

(PIGAFETTA *walks wearily across the deck and sits on a barrel.*)

PIGAFETTA	The months roll by . . . (*opening book and turning pages back*) 'On WEDNESDAY, 28th NOVEMBER in the year 1520, we left the Strait of Storms and entered the Pacific Sea.' (*He laughs.*) And to think that when we saw the Peaceful Sea and cried 'Pacifico!' we thought our troubles were all over.

(HENRIQUE *walks slowly in and sinks down beside Pigafetta.*)

HENRIQUE	What can you find to make you laugh, Great Master of the Book?
PIGAFETTA	So that's what you call me, Henrique! (*looking round*) But where's your master! I've never known you leave his side before.
HENRIQUE	(*giving a half laugh*) There's not a man on board with enough strength to lift a dagger – let alone harm Master Magellan.
PIGAFETTA	I heard you laugh! Tell me, what can a slave find to laugh at?

HENRIQUE	I laugh at life, good Master Pigafetta – while I have some left. (*He lifts his arms and flops back.*)
PIGAFETTA	You are a wise fellow, Henrique, and serve your master well. (*thoughtfully*) No one but the Admiral Magellan could have brought us through such terrible hardships. (*He turns pages of book on.*)
HENRIQUE	You write in that great book each day, my Lord! (*curiously*) What do you find to say?
PIGAFETTA	This is the story of the voyage. I had meant to give it to the King when we returned to Spain, but now . . .
HENRIQUE	(*giving a half laugh*) But now you think you've done it all for nothing . . . because we shall not return?
PIGAFETTA	Perhaps! Yesterday I wrote . . . (*reads*) 'Never again will any man undertake to make such a voyage.'
HENRIQUE	What else do you put in your book . . . (*grinning*) After all . . . one day you will give it to the King!
PIGAFETTA	(*turning one page back*) Two days ago I wrote . . . 'We have remained three months and twenty days without taking provisions or fresh water on board . . . we have eaten only old biscuits turned to powder, all full of worms . . . and drunk only yellow, stinking water . . . We have eaten ox hides . . . and chewed the rigging of the ships. And of the rats – we could not get enough . . .'
	(RICARDO *and* RAPHAEL *stagger in, supporting each other.*)
RICARDO	RATS! Did you say RATS?
RAPHAEL	(*taking coin from pocket*) My last ecu, but I'll give it all for one small rat!
	(BRUNO *comes in holding up a rat's tail.*)

BRUNO	I have a rat's tail here! How much for the tail?
RICARDO	Is it tender, Bruno?
RAPHAEL	Let's share it out. (*laughing*) How many of us are there?
RICARDO	(*counting*) Five!
BRUNO	(*measuring tail*) Then we will need to make five equal parts.
HENRIQUE	I shall not eat all mine at once!
	(*A loud clang is heard.*)
ALL	What's that?
HENRIQUE	Ah! (*He pulls himself to his feet and struggles out.*)
BRUNO	Even the slave can hardly find enough strength to walk.
RICARDO	I didn't hear Magellan call.
RAPHAEL	Perhaps he is too weak. He's suffered with us all!
RICARDO	He has a will of iron – that man.
RAPHAEL	(*nodding*) Only the Admiral could have brought us through so far.
	(HENRIQUE *comes in dangling large rat by tail.*)
HENRIQUE	See! Caught in my trap!
RICARDO	So that was what we heard!
RAPHAEL	(*pointing to rat*) Look at the size of him!
BRUNO	(*taking coins from pocket*) How much for him, Henrique? Will you take two ecu?
HENRIQUE	A prize like this cannot be bought for money. We'll share him . . . with the tail . . . between the five of us.
VOICE OF ELCANO	LAND AHOY! LAND AHOY!
ALL	(*disbelievingly*) LAND! (*They stagger to side and look out.*)

HENRIQUE	I'll to my master. (*He goes out.*)
RICARDO	Water! We shall have fresh water . . .
RAPHAEL	. . . and provisions!
PIGAFETTA	(*cautiously*) Perhaps we should hold back our hopes a little while. Remember those Islands of Misfortune, where we could not find an anchorage!
BRUNO	If needs be, I'll swim ashore and eat the trees and grass!
	(MAGELLAN *comes in, followed by* HENRIQUE *and* ELCANO.)
MAGELLAN	We've sighted land! (*thoughtfully*) Three months and eight days upon this ocean – without a single storm – but now we've sighted land.
PIGAFETTA	You rightly named this sea, 'PACIFIC', my Lord Admiral.
ELCANO	(*pointing*) There are small boats being rowed towards us, so we've reached a resting place. (*to Pigafetta*) What is the day, good scribe?
PIGAFETTA	WEDNESDAY the 6th of MARCH in the year one thousand, five hundred and twenty-one. (*taking out quill*) We've reached some islands, which we hope are friendly! I'll write it down.
	(PIGAFETTA *goes out and* ELCANO *moves to side and watches.*)
MAGELLAN	Man the forward watch, Ricardo! To your places, men!
SEAMEN	Aye, aye, Admiral! (*They move forward and out.*)
ELCANO	There are a great number of little canoe-boats, Admiral. They're being rowed hard towards us.
MAGELLAN	Do they carry weapons?

ELCANO It seems not, but they're packed tight with natives . . . There are so many . . . and they're coming close alongside.

(*Yells and cries are heard as* RICARDO *runs in.*)

RICARDO (*breathless from his effort*) The natives . . . are trying . . . to board us!

MAGELLAN (*hurrying to side to look out*) Then fight them off!

RICARDO Lord Admiral! They're fit and strong . . . and we are . . . so weak. (*He falls to the deck.*)

(RAPHAEL *hurries in.*)

RAPHAEL Admiral! These natives swarm like ants!

(BRUNO *comes in.*)

BRUNO They've taken our small boat which we had fastened to the poop deck!

MAGELLAN (*pulling dagger*) Then we will have it back!

(MAGELLAN *strides out, followed by* HENRIQUE *and* SEAMEN *supporting* RICARDO.)

ELCANO (*ruefully*) Three months and twenty days at sea and we reach an island . . . full of thieves! (*He follows others out.*)

     ★   ★   ★   ★   ★

(PIGAFETTA *walks cheerfully across the deck carrying his Journal.*)

PIGAFETTA How life has changed since we left the Islands of Thieves and sailed on to Cebu. (*He opens book and reads.*) 'We are well fed and much restored to health . . .' (*looking up*) . . . as you now see!

(RICARDO, RAPHAEL *and* BRUNO *come in, carrying a large bunch of bananas.*)

RICARDO Look what we have here!

RAPHAEL Ricardo says they're some kind of fig.

BRUNO   But they're too long and yellow.

RICARDO   (*to Pigafetta*) You are a man of learning, Great Master of the Book. What do you say they are?

PIGAFETTA   (*peeling back skin*) What do the people of these islands do with them?

RAPHAEL   Eat them!

PIGAFETTA   Then we will do the same.

(ALL *skin and eat bananas.*)

BRUNO   Write in your book that . . . Ricardo, Raphael . . . and good Bruno, found a new fruit which was very good to eat!

RICARDO   (*rubbing hands together*) How else can we be put into your book, Master?

PIGAFETTA   (*laughing*) What brave deeds have you done?

RAPHAEL   The Admiral does the deeds!

BRUNO   (*curiously*) What do you write about the Admiral Magellan, good Master?

PIGAFETTA   (*carefully*) Well . . . (*turning back one page*) . . . what did I write yesterday? (*reads*) 'The Captain General, Admiral Magellan, returned to our ship, Vittoria, with the treaty he had this day made with the King of these Islands, the largest of which is named Cebu.' (*looking up*) So now we shall have peace!

(MAGELLAN *hurries in carrying a scroll.*)

MAGELLAN   Not so, it seems!

PIGAFETTA   Why is that?

MAGELLAN   The natives of these islands may be at peace with us on paper . . . (*tapping scroll*) but it seems they still play games . . . with arrows!

ALL   (*scornfully*) With ARROWS!

MAGELLAN	ARROWS . . . tipped with POISON! I sent Elcano, some two hours ago, to burn down the houses of the ones who do it. That should frighten them!
	(ELCANO *hurries in.*)
ELCANO	My Lord Admiral! We burned some thirty huts, as you commanded. But now all hell has broken out!
MAGELLAN	(*waving scroll*) So much for this treaty with the King! I'll teach these natives a lesson they won't forget. (*to Ricardo, Raphael and Bruno*) Gather our fighting men! (*They run out.*) Now . . . (*thoughtfully*) who else can come with me?
ELCANO	I'll come, my Lord Admiral!
MAGELLAN	No! Take my place here, Elcano, and I'll take . . . Cam, Gaspar and Cabral!
	(MAGELLAN *strides out.*)
PIGAFETTA	(*sadly*) It seems that we are not meant to stay here in peace, Elcano.
ELCANO	(*pointing*) It was war out there! They shot their arrows at our legs. I never thought I could run so fast!
PIGAFETTA	What other weapons do these natives have?
ELCANO	Lances, made of bamboo . . . and STONES! You should have seen the stones! (*rubs shoulder*) And felt them!
PIGAFETTA	It's the arrows I would be afraid of.
ELCANO	I'm afraid for the Admiral. He is so bold!
PIGAFETTA	You speak as his loyal captain now, Elcano. Tell me! What do you hope to gain . . . when we are back in Spain?

ELCANO	(*quickly*) A KNIGHTHOOD! (*slowly*) I've always wanted that. You are a Knight of Rhodes. If the King would make me Knight . . . of Seville . . . I'd be well satisfied!
PIGAFETTA	That will come your way, Elcano. You have proved yourself.
	(*Cries are heard as* HENRIQUE *is carried on deck by* RICARDO, RAPHAEL *and* BRUNO.)
RICARDO	(*breathlessly*) We've been sent back with Henrique . . . on the Admiral's orders.
ELCANO	Where is he wounded?
HENRIQUE	(*raising head*) An arrow, captain.
RAPHAEL	It's gone deep into his leg.
BRUNO	And must be got out, captain.
ELCANO	Hold him!
HENRIQUE	(*gritting teeth*) Do what you must.
	(RICARDO, RAPHAEL *and* BRUNO *hold down* HENRIQUE, *as* ELCANO *pulls out arrow*.)
ELCANO	(*holding arrow in air*) I have it here!
HENRIQUE	(*raising head*) My thanks . . . UGH! (*He sinks back*.)
RICARDO	(*looking down at Henrique*) A strong man.
RAPHAEL	Not a whimper from him.
BRUNO	(*shaking Henrique*) Come Henrique! The captain has the arrow out.
ELCANO	(*on knees beside Henrique*) Suck out the poison from his wound . . . like this! (ELCANO *sucks and spits*.) Take him below!
	(RICARDO, RAPHAEL *and* BRUNO *carry* HENRIQUE *out*.)
PIGAFETTA	Do you think that the good Henrique will live, Elcano?

69

ELCANO (*shrugging*) I know nothing of these native poisons. But I'd like to know what's going on out there. (*He moves to side and looks out.*)

PIGAFETTA The valiant Admiral will put those natives down. (*He goes out.*)

ELCANO Pray God that Pigafetta's words are true.

(ELCANO *turns round as* CAM, GASPAR *and* CABRAL *walk slowly in, bow heads, and pull cloaks over faces.*)

What does this mean? (*hurrying forward*) Cam! Gaspar! Cabral! Speak!

(*Silence*)

(*in horror*) Your silence tells me what I fear to know.

CAM MAGELLAN IS DEAD!

(*Silence*)

ELCANO What happened?

GASPAR (*taking deep breath*) The Admiral was brought down . . . first by a bamboo lance which struck his face and arm . . .

CABRAL He called out, 'I'll hold them! Get back to the ship!'

CAM Which is what we began to do . . . It was a command . . . But then they fell upon him.

GASPAR Hearing him call out like that, they knew he was the leader.

CABRAL The next blow cut his legs from underneath his body . . .

CAM He fell . . . face downwards . . . DEAD!

GASPAR But not before he called out a second time.

CABRAL	This time he called out, 'Leave me here. Get back to the ship.'
CAM	And so they slew our LIGHT . . .
GASPAR	. . . our COMFORT . . .
CABRAL	. . . and our true GUIDE.
ALL	God rest his soul! AMEN! (*They make the sign of the cross and file out with heads bowed and murmuring,* 'God rest his soul.')

★   ★   ★   ★   ★

(PIGAFETTA *walks slowly across the deck, holding his Journal. He sits on a barrel.*)

PIGAFETTA	(*sighing*) 27th APRIL. It was a dark day for us when Magellan fell. (*opening book*) What did I write in here? (*reads*) 'May the fame of so valiant a Captain of the Seas never be forgotten. Among his virtues . . . He was strong in danger . . . He endured terrible hunger better than all the others . . . He was great in knowledge and skill . . .' (*looking up*) And no other man should have the credit for being FIRST to sail round the world!

(*Enter* ELCANO.)

ELCANO	Pigafetta! Ho there! I need your advice.
PIGAFETTA	(*surprised*) Do you, Elcano? Since you took command we have not seen you waver!
ELCANO	(*confidentially*) I must appear bold – like Magellan did. But now . . . I'm not sure which way to go.
PIGAFETTA	(*unbelievingly*) Not sure which way to go?
ELCANO	(*pointing*) Out there are Portuguese ships! They'll try to board us when they see our Spanish flag.
PIGAFETTA	That's true, Elcano . . . . but we are *all* in this. Why don't you ask the other captains?

ELCANO	(*anxiously*) How can I ask their counsel and still be in command? Suppose they disagree?
PIGAFETTA	You can put it to the other captains. And if they disagree – DRAW LOTS!
ELCANO	DRAW LOTS! That's it! Call Cam, Gaspar, and Cabral!
PIGAFETTA	I'll do that. (*He hurries out.*)
ELCANO	(*thoughtfully*) There must be an uneven number when we draw. This Pigafetta is the wisest of us all. I'll have him in it.
	(CAM, GASPAR *and* CABRAL *come in, followed by* PIGAFETTA.)
ELCANO	Ho there, captains!
CAM	What do you want with us?
ELCANO	Let's put our heads together . . . COMRADES!
CAPTAINS	COMRADES! (*They look suspiciously at each other.*)
GASPAR	You call us 'Comrades', and ask us for our counsel!
CABRAL	What's wrong? Is the ship holed?
ELCANO	Not yet! But that could happen soon. (*pointing*) Your brothers are out there!
CAPTAINS	BROTHERS!
ELCANO	Your Portuguese brothers are out there in their men-of-war. They'll try to board us when they see our Spanish flag.
CAM	(*to other captains*) Elcano is right!
PIGAFETTA	We're weak, after these three long years at sea, and they'll be strong.
ELCANO	So . . . which way home to Spain? (*taking out chart and pointing*) Look! We are here.

GASPAR   We should keep away from Africa. The Portuguese will be along da Gama's route to India.

CABRAL   (*disagreeing*) But we are too weak to sail the high seas. We should keep CLOSE to Africa, I say.

ELCANO   That's the problem, captains. Do we sail close by the coast and hope that the Portuguese in their men-of-war won't see us, or make for the Green Islands farther to the west?

PIGAFETTA   Elcano has it in mind to draw lots on which way to go. You are all in it, captains.

ELCANO   And so are you, good Pigafetta.

(PIGAFETTA *bows.*)

PIGAFETTA   Here are the straws! (*Taking straws from tunic pocket*) Short ones for Africa (*giving one to each*) . . . and long for a voyage out to the Green Islands in the west. (*giving one straw to each and taking off hat*) I'll put my hat down here. And now we'll turn our backs.

CAM   Turn our backs?

GASPAR   Why should we do that?

CABRAL   (*pointing to hat*) The hat is here!

PIGAFETTA   We turn our backs so that no man knows how his comrades cast their votes. (ALL CAPTAINS *turn backs.*) I'll put my straw in first! And then I'll throw the one I didn't use into the waters! Now . . . Cam! (CAM *puts straw in hat and throws other away.*) Gaspar! (GASPAR *does the same.*) Next . . . Cabral! (CABRAL *does the same.*) . . . Elcano! (ELCANO *does the same.*) We're done!

(ALL THREE CAPTAINS *look eagerly into hat.*)

CAM   There are FOUR – for the long way round . . .

GASPAR   . . . by the Green Islands!

CABRAL	(*disappointed*) I would have preferred Africa!
PIGAFETTA	This is a secret ballot, captains! But . . . (*holding up straws*) it's FOUR to ONE! You have your answer, Elcano.
ELCANO	We sail north-west from here! But if we are seen by any of the Portuguese, we'll make a run for it! Agreed?
CAPTAINS	Agreed!
ELCANO	Let's go!

(CAPTAINS *go out, but* ELCANO *pauses and comes back to Pigafetta.*)

Write it in your great book, good Scribe, that Elcano consulted with his captains. (*He goes out.*)

PIGAFETTA	(*sits down, opens book and writes*) '11th JULY 1522 . . . This day Captain Elcano consulted with the other Captains . . .' (*looking up*) It is the first time I have written that! (*thoughtfully*) Now . . . how shall I end my journal for the King? (*writes*) 'Your Majesty will judge us . . . on the merit in that we sailed ROUND the world . . . and that having departed from the WEST . . . we returned from the EAST.' (*standing up*) And by the grace of God we shall soon be home again!

(PIGAFETTA *walks out slowly, carrying Journal.*)

END OF THIRD PLAY

 **PLAYWATCHERS**

Spanish Monks

BARTHOLOMEW	And so they were! Some two months later, Elcano brought Vittoria into the harbour at Seville.
FRANCISCO	Elcano! Tell me, Bartholomew! Did Elcano get his knighthood?
PAULO	Was he made Lord of Seville?
BARTHOLOMEW	No! He died a disappointed man, but he was loyal to Magellan's memory. He wrote . . . in here . . . (*opening another book*) . . . 'Magellan of GLORIOUS MEMORY . . .'
FRANCISCO	So 'The Fox' won him over!
PAULO	He did! Magellan had his faults! (*laughing*) At least, those Spanish Captains must have thought so!
BARTHOLOMEW	But never let it be forgotten what Magellan DID. He linked Columbus' route west, with da Gama's to the east.
FRANCISCO	And no other man should have the credit for being FIRST, to sail around . . . (*tapping*) this globe . . .
PAULO	(*spinning globe back*) . . . although his body lies here . . . (*pointing*) in the East Indies. Bartholomew! What will you do now?
BARTHOLOMEW	(*clasping Pigafetta's Journal*) PRINT THIS BOOK! The Knight of Rhodes, the good Pigafetta, who wrote this and survived those three

terrible years, must also have HIS place in history.

FRANCISCO   (*curiously*) I do believe that you admire him as much as any of the Admirals, Bartholomew!

BARTHOLOMEW   (*thoughtfully*) I think I do . . . (*opening book*) Hear how the journal ends . . . 'I will now go to the King with this book, written each day in my own hand of all things done upon the voyage. This he will prize above gold and silver.' (*He closes book and goes out.*)

FRANCISCO   Come, Brother Paulo! This is a good note upon which to end our tale.

PAULO   What Pigafetta wrote is true. There ARE more things to prize on Earth than gold!

(*They both go out, carrying books.*)

Off we sail on the Santa Gabriel

Traditional windlass and capstan shanty

Off we sail on the San - ta Ga - bri - el,

Off we sail on the San - ta Ga - bri - el,

Off we sail on the San - ta Ga - bri - el

On the way to for - tune! Heave - ho! And

up she ri - ses, Heave - ho! And up she ri - ses,

Heave - ho! And up she ri - ses

on the way to for - tune!

Suggestions for the Playmakers

The outline of the ship can be set up quickly with barrels or boxes (obtained from your local greengrocer). Screw hooks into opposite sides. Bind curtain hooks onto the ends of rope or strong cord, and loop these over the hooks.

Make a flag to name each ship.

Make stores for the ships.

Stuff old sacks with light-weight materials.

Paint cardboard cartons from supermarkets to look like wooden boxes and chests.

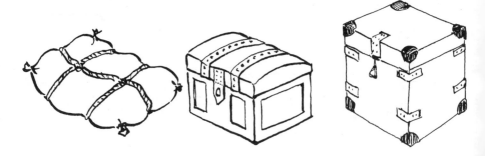

If you are a ship's officer in one of the plays, you could dress like this.

If you are a seaman in one of the plays, you could dress like this.

You could make a Recorder's head-dress like this.

Wind two scarves around each other. Sew them onto an old woolly hat with one end hanging down.

You could make fifteenth-century navigation instruments out of strong cardboard.

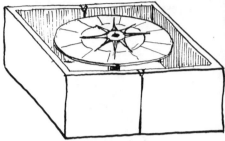

Early compasses were kept in boxes called binnacles.

An astrolabe measures the angular distance of sun and stars. This is used to calculate the latitude of the ship.

Make an hour-glass by putting an egg-timer into an open-sided box so it can be carried.

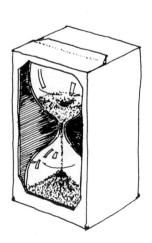

Make a cross staff in wood or strong card.

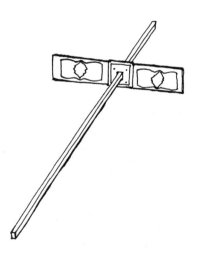